T0132285

Who Knew
Life Could Be This Good

Your personality is the secret to a happier and healthier life.

DR. WILLIAM MEHRING

BALBOA.PRESS
A DIVISION OF HAY HOUSE

Balboa Press books may be ordered through booksellers or by contacting:

Balboa Press
A Division of Hay House
1663 Liberty Drive
Bloomington, IN 47403
www.balboapress.com
1 (877) 407-4847

Because of the dynamic nature of the Internet, any web addresses or links contained in this book may have changed since publication and may no longer be valid. The views expressed in this work are solely those of the author and do not necessarily reflect the views of the publisher, and the publisher hereby disclaims any responsibility for them.

The author of this book does not dispense medical advice or prescribe the use of any technique as a form of treatment for physical, emotional, or medical problems without the advice of a physician, either directly or indirectly. The intent of the author is only to offer information of a general nature to help you in your quest for emotional and spiritual well-being. In the event you use any of the information in this book for yourself, which is your constitutional right, the author and the publisher assume no responsibility for your actions.

ISBN: 978-1-9822-4475-0 (sc)
ISBN: 978-1-9822-4474-3 (e)

Library of Congress Control Number: 2020904771

Print information available on the last page.

Balboa Press rev. date: 03/30/2020

Contents

E3 Emotional Energetic Evolution Therapy:
A Roadmap to Discovering and Creating
The Life You Never Imagined Possible

The Undeniable Link Between Stress and Dis-ease:

We all have stress in our lives every day. Did you know that stress is the main cause of our mental, emotional, and even physical anxieties and diseases? There is a direct relationship between one's emotional health and one's physical health, pain, and/or disease. In this presentation you will discover your personality type and how to utilize your unique strengths to manage your stress, fears, and frustrations to restore health and joy in your life. By learning to utilize proven strategies to avoid your specific stress triggers, and discovering coping mechanisms for handling stress, you will gain control over your physical and emotional evolution. As you understand and engage in this process in a deep way you will become capable of great self-healing.

Before we begin this journey I would like to introduce myself and explain how my practice evolved from the utilization of a wide range of chiropractic techniques including adjustments, applied kinesiology, and massage therapy to a blend of physical and emotional medicine which accesses the subconscious mind and diagnoses the heart of the emotional problem/s which are contributing to your physical pain or disease.

It was as a chiropractic doctor that I first began to understand the physical effects of stress. Most of my clients who had strained their backs could easily be healed with one to three weeks of treatment, stretches and exercises. Off they would go not to be seen by me again until they overextended themselves as weekend warriors. However, I also had patients who kept coming back from time to time for pain in the same area. I puzzled over why I could not eradicate this problem through treatment, some new ergonomics, stretches and/or exercises. As I worked on the muscles, connective tissues, and skeletal components to help alleviate their pain, these patients often began talking about stressful things in their lives. Obviously there was a connection. I decided to allocate some time to just sit with a few of these patients and ask them to explore what was triggering their feelings of stress. The patients who were the best at seeing the issues at hand and their roles in the situations were also the most capable of releasing the pain and dysfunction in their bodies. Oftentimes I would not see these patients again because the source of the pain had been dealt with and their bodies regained balance. When I would see them later in town, they thanked me deeply for spending that extra time with them getting to the root of their problems.

For years doctors have known that people under stress commonly express their stress through their neurological and muscular skeletal systems. It's common knowledge that many people experience headaches and neck or back pain when they are stressed. Other stress induced symptoms range from irritable bowel syndrome, acidic stomach, heart palpitations and a multitude of other medical conditions. Our physical bodies and health are a direct reflection of our emotional health. Constant emotional work is one of the most important pieces of the puzzle needed for good health. The most important thing you can do for your health is to choose to keep your emotional state balanced, positive, and healthy. It is most important that you begin right away to integrate new habits that will create the new you. You have the capacity to affect the most important part of your health and happiness. This journey of emotional evolution and harmonization may seem difficult because it is new to you, however it will be the most rewarding work of your life.

I am sure that you have come here to learn about this program for many different reasons. Some of you may be here to learn how to prevent the destructive effects of stress, some might be looking for a way to expand their experiences of joy and gratitude in life, while others may wish to add emotional work as one of the most important tools used to cope and fight disease. I would like to share with you some of my own experiences and discoveries, and a case history to give you a greater understanding of how I got here and began helping others heal themselves through the deep emotional work that saved my life.

My Personal Evolution:

After working twelve years in my chiropractic practice, I suffered a vestibular injury which altered my balance and left me with chronic exertion headaches. Suffering from pain and poor balance, it was impossible for me to continue my chiropractic work, which was my passion. I had to figure out another way to live a happy, productive life. My true learning began during the subsequent four years, which turned out to be the most disharmonious years I've ever experienced.

First, I opened a boat dealership, a seasonal business requiring long hours and a frenzied pace. This brought out my competitive nature as I strove to outsell all the other boat dealers. Boat manufacturers reward dealers who have the highest sales regardless of their tactics or work ethics, so even my moral compass was challenged in this environment. If I lost a deal to another boat dealership, I would become upset. Striving for financial success, I pushed harder to close more deals. I became progressively more angry and my behavior more cutthroat. As a competitive person and chiropractor, I was no stranger to the body's stress response, but this new work environment was the epitome of stress combined with chaos. It brought out issues of inferiority—feelings of not being good enough and not being valued. I could not find inner peace no matter how hard I tried.

Outwardly, everything looked great. I was successful, confident and seemingly on top of the world. I received many awards for the highest sales per capita and the highest customer service satisfaction ratings of all the dealerships for this boat manufacturer. Unfortunately, all this was fueled by fear and I lived in a constant state of trying to prove to myself and to the world that I was good enough, acceptable, and lovable. I had very little time with my wife and baby, and lost most of my friends. Even worse, I was unable to see all of this happening.

Eventually everything backfired. Instead of fixing the problem that I was trying to escape, I created the very thing I feared: the feeling that I was not good enough. In my blindness to my dysfunctional belief system and addiction to wrong actions, I said and did things that created more chaos in my life. My ego was in control of my life. This part of our conscious mind has good traits and bad traits. For most of us, it is the ego that gets us up in the morning and gets us off to work so that we can make money, and provide for ourselves and family. It is the motivation that most people use to run their lives; however when the ego tries to remedy what it fears it creates actions that can potentially lead to obsessive-compulsive behaviors. Sadly, this is the way of it. When we are engaged in the needs of the ego and striving to fill the vast emptiness of ego, we rarely see the damaging effects of our destructive actions. We don't see our part in the stress we create in our lives or take responsibility for the effect we have on the people around us. On some level, I knew that I had to change and transform my beliefs and actions in order to save my life and my relationships.

One day while working late, I received a revelation from deep within, "You are killing yourself!" I knew it was true. I went to work the next day and announced to everyone that I would be selling the business. This came as a shock to everyone, especially my business partner, with whom I had to resolve many differences. However, the phone soon rang with an offer to purchase the dealership. The boat dealership sold, and my partner became an employee of the new owner. I was free, but that freedom came with a weighty responsibility. I had to deal with my fears and was forced to resolve my issues of self-worth, and my need for productivity, control, and acceptance. I had to restructure my beliefs, personal values, and other significant elements in my life, but how?

Then I discovered I could begin my healing process by rechanneling my productive and competitive nature within the framework of athletics. Since I could no longer be a competitive water skier due to my vestibular injury, I began to physically work hard on swimming and cycling. Soon I joined a group of people training for triathlons. I enjoyed the comradery and the training. Then I was introduced to Qi gong. This traditional Taoist practice incorporates intention, meditation, relaxation, physical movement, mind-body integration, and breathing exercises. I began to bring my life's unhealthy patterns to the forefront of my awareness so that I could engage with and transform them knowing that my very life depended upon this work.

As part of the triathlon training, I rode my bike deep into the backcountry and then ran on a trail along a river. Once I was deep under the canopy of the Oaks and Sycamore trees, I would sit and meditate on simply receiving. I cleared my mind, grounded myself in the five senses and the sensations of living. Purple, magenta and green colors appeared before my closed eyes. I began to feel a greater awareness of the infinite energetic field of which I was a part. As I experienced the complete absence of "doing," the complete presence of receiving grew larger and larger. Much to my surprise, I began to see that many of the events and interactions of my life were unhealthy. Each time I envisioned something I needed to transform, I would seek out the person involved and I'd say to them, "I did something to you that I didn't like. If I were to do it over today, this is how I would behave today." Once I started this process, I was compelled to continue this spring cleaning for my soul. This important process of receiving and repenting changed my life on many levels.

This deep introspection became a habit for me and it was a habit that became self-perpetuating because it led to harmonization and healing. I believe that healing ones deepest wounds is the sweetest nectar of life. I also believe you can heal or harmonize any situation that has occurred in your life at any time and the result will be the same whether you work on it immediately after the situation occured or years later. It's never too late, but we must be mindful of the tendency to procrastinate. Procrastination can steal away the life you long for. We often come up with logical, if not honorable, reasons to not embrace our fears. We tend to look for excuses for our behavior and actions. Sadly people on their deathbed feel compelled to tell their family and friends about the things they wish they would have said or done differently. Sometimes it takes the death process to see that the most important thing in life is to express our inner truth and affection and not run away from our fears.

Six months into my process of self introspection and healing, my wife convinced me to see a dermatologist to evaluate a freckle on my chest that had grown dramatically over the last year and half. The dermatologist recommended removal and biopsy. After the procedure he called with the results, indicating there was good news and bad news. I asked if I could hear the bad news first hoping to end the conversation on an upbeat note. The doctor told me the bad news was that the biopsy confirmed malignant melanoma, but the good news was that the disease looked as if it was going through a rare spontaneous remission, which is uncommon for this type of skin cancer. The dermatologist also said that there were no signs of malignant tentacles spreading from the skin cancer and that the freckle might disappear on its own in a couple of months. I was taught, at that time, that stage three or four malignant melanoma had roughly a 5% five-year survival rate, but the pathologist report indicated the remission process had begun about six months earlier. The doctor asked, "What have you been doing differently recently?" I told him about the emotional work I began six months earlier and he recommended I keep it up.

I followed this advice and ultimately realized I had to return to my passion as a healer. Since I could no longer be a chiropractor, I returned to graduate school for a Master's degree in psychology and philosophy, and further training in homeopathy and hypnotherapy. I also took classes in comparative religion.

My Eyes Were Opened—Disease Can Be Temporary

Everything changed for me one day in a psychology class when we were watching a film on a woman with multiple personality disorder. This seemingly inconsequential film had me riveted. I was particularly interested in her case and the manifestations of her two distinct personalities. I was fascinated that whenever she shifted from one personality to the other, her physical appearance changed dramatically as well. There were demonstrative morphological changes in her posture, facial expression, and gait. What wasn't clear to me then, but is very clear to me now, was that these physical changes were in response to the changes in her thoughts, beliefs, interactions with life events, and view of herself. Her two personalities reacted differently to the same life events depending on which personality was present. The two different personalities interpreted the same events in different ways both physically and emotionally. Each personality had its own unique beliefs, language, morals and triggers. In one of her personalities she had irregularities in her heart and a murmur that was the result of these irregularities. When she became embedded in her other personality she had the symptoms of systemic lupus erythematosus. Her blood work would even change the longer she was in that personality. It became clear to me that her "disease" was a direct result of the personality she was in and the filters through which she saw and reacted to her life's events. So the exciting news here is that disease is clearly temporary. There is great flexibility in our bodies and ultimately the outcome of our physical status is based on our personality and how it perceives the world around us. This was the first big step in my realization that our body's health is a reflection of our emotional wellbeing.

I have always been fascinated by the world of quantum mechanics and all of the experimentation that has revealed how consciousness when wrapped around the potential of undifferentiated energy that makes up subatomic particles shapes physical reality. This is all entirely possible in the knowledge of our quantum world where everything that is matter and physical is made of energy. This is what gives amazing flexibility to the physical makeup of our bodies and the world around us—the place where physics interfaces with the real world of psychology and human health. **This startling realization forced me** to ponder how our rigid thought patterns keep us from understanding the true potential of our identity and our healing abilities.

Nurture vs. Nature…. Nature Wins

The phenomenon of twins has always been of particular interest to me. They provide a real life experiment that can tell us a lot about how our DNA works as well as the origins of our personality, spirit and perhaps our soul. Whenever I have met a set of identical twins, I've asked them questions about their similarities and differences in personality, physicality and common ailments or diseases. The first thing that became very apparent was that identical twins, even though they shared the same placenta and should therefore be absolutely identical, began developing unique features and personalities very early on. Looking at early pictures of the twins, when they were available, revealed that they began to develop different responses and unique qualities at a very early age. They began to look a little different. As I investigated their personalities through either questioning or tests, they were always different. Even though they had experienced the same events, they took away very different memories and interpretations. The two twins had completely different emotional responses because they had two distinct personalities. Emotional traumas are very powerful and can date back to as early as the second trimester of maturation. As time went by and they became older their unique differences continued to develop. It is easy for parents and really good friends to tell the differences between twins, because they can see the little physical and personality changes that have been created throughout their lives.

Epigenetic science predicts that these changes will indeed happen. During development in the womb and after birth, our surroundings, exposures, and nutrition influence how our genes are expressed and how our bodies and minds develop. For example, two identical twins may have the same genes for height, but if one twin does not receive the same amount of nutrients while in the womb, it may be shorter than the other twin. We all build up mutations in our DNA over time. What we see is that the DNA of twins begins changing as soon as the soul and personality are embedded in the young developing fetus. In my work I have found that the soonest this can occur is the second trimester. As soon as the soul and personality are embedded in the developing child the DNA begins to change in response to its experiences. Each defining moment that triggers an intense enough response in our emotional world, whether positive or negative, influences and remodels our DNA and runs through the filter of our personality. This in turn brings about adaptive changes in our DNA and therefore our physical makeup. These changes over the long-term may have positive or possibly negative consequences.

The next striking reality is that our personality, spirit and soul are not completely tethered to our DNA. If this was the case all twins would be identical in nearly all aspects of life. Each of us is unique with our own capacities, obstacles, and gifts in life. Most exciting is that we have the absolute freedom to decide how we will interpret each defining moment in our life and hopefully then make most of the events in our life positive ones so that we continue to nurture and protect our DNA. If you don't think you have choices in life, think again. Although you may not have choices in the events that bring difficult challenges and lessons, you have the undisputed ability to interpret them and work with them in such a way that you can create the most positive outcomes possible. You can make the best of any situation in your life. We do our best work when we process the events of our life and move forward. A good goal is to cherish the joys of life as well as the lessons we learn from life's obstacles. **When you are on this path of harmonizing your belief systems you have the greatest potential for a joyous and healthy life.**

Our Physical Health—A Reflection of Our Emotional State

It is important to understand how our body works and the intimate relationship between our emotions and our physical health. Our body and emotions are constantly in flux and our decisions have the greatest influence on these changes. It is quite fair to say that our physical makeup is a direct reflection of our emotional status. The traditional model in years past has been that there exist genes in your body that make you susceptible to disease including cancer. These genes would be triggered by toxins, carcinogens or ionizing radiation. What we know now is that emotional trauma is also an important player or trigger. If you feel good and life is on track your body is constantly regenerating itself. If on the other hand your life is stressful, filled with dissatisfaction, anger or is in a constant state of contention, then you will be accelerating the effects of aging and inhibiting your natural healing ability to thwart off disease.

Let us now look into the building blocks of our thoughts and consciousness. When you feel stressed, every cell in your body can and will feel stressed. What we have learned through nanotechnology is that **each cell of your body has a unique consciousness.** This is to say that your thoughts are influenced by each and every cell in your body. We can no longer say that the brain controls all of our thoughts. There is a constant interplay between the cells of your body and your brain. The brain acts as the central hub for the input of information throughout your body. The interesting part of this communication is that it occurs through something that is known as the "Field", which is nothing more than a Wi-Fi system. It's really quite simple, this field surrounds the body and all of the cells of your body communicate through information that is held in coherent light waveforms just like information is held in radio waveforms. Coherent light is an amazing phenomenon in nature. Laser light is a form of coherent light. This light source does not break down the same way conventional light or radio waves do. This allows clean information to be transmitted throughout the body. This light carries within it information and the state of your emotional and physical well-being. The good news is that when there is an unhealthy condition or something in your body needs to be healed, all of the cells of your body are working as a collective. The bad news is that when you are unhappy, distressed and having unhealthy emotions all of the cells of your body will be adversely affected. This is one of the most important reasons why choosing what your thoughts will be is imperative for good health. Every day we wake up and take a shower to clean our body, brush our teeth, and eat the right foods, but the most important thing that we can do for our health is choose to keep our emotional state clean and healthy. This is where you can have the greatest influence on your long-term health and the quality of the joy you will feel in your day-to-day life. Quite often we take our health for granted until it begins to diminish. Constant emotional work is one of the most important pieces of the puzzle needed for good health. It is delicious and self-perpetuating as you unload all of the baggage you have carried through much of your life. This work is the only action in your life that will lead to perpetual joy. Once I experienced the journey of an emotional evolution and harmonization, I realized it was time to begin helping others.

Throughout my personal journey of discovery and healing I learned four basic truths:

- First, there is an internal wisdom inside each of us which speaks from the subconscious mind helping us stay on a beneficial path of mental and physical health. I am inclined to call that intelligence our soul, but many call it our subconscious. Chiropractic philosophy uses this innate intelligence and the role of muscle testing to penetrate deep into our memories to help us determine the origins and emotional issues that create our stress. Applied kinesiology, a chiropractic technique that utilizes the strength of muscles, weak or strong, can help direct the doctor to find the treatment or nutrition necessary to return a patient to optimum health.

- Second, discovering and exposing my fears, weaknesses, and wrongdoings was empowering. I thought I would feel weak, but instead I felt strong. No longer susceptible to personal judgment, I felt WHOLE, in sync with my need to re-create myself and perhaps my life's path. While doing this work I began to see the world through my soul and not my ego. The result being, I have accepted and embraced who I am. Rather than following my ego, which is always comparing itself to others, and amplifying my perceived weaknesses, I connect with and listen to my soul. When in this healing process, all negative and destructive thoughts and actions disappear.

- Third, I realized that all my priorities and beliefs that were linked to unharmonious actions needed to be changed! I also realized that in order for my beliefs to change,

I had to challenge them by altering my actions that had brought me stress in the past. If I was unsure of what action to take, I found that the best action was doing the exact opposite of what I had done before. As a result of this process, I realized that the most important thing for me to do in life was to constantly be aware of my motivations for each of my actions. I was no longer afraid to see my thoughts because they were indications of where I needed to work.

- Fourth, and most importantly, I realized from my experience that disease need not be permanent. Our physical health is a reflection of our emotional health.

The journey of emotional evolution and harmonization may seem difficult, but perhaps that's only because you have not done the work before. If you are of the belief that power and material items are what will bring you happiness, ask yourself to look at how long a new car or a diamond ring brought you internal peace not to mention better health. The most important part is that you begin the process immediately and do not put it off until tomorrow or next week or sometime that will never come. Our tendency as humans is to repeat what we have done in the past. When you start this process today you will have created a new habit. The process of change starts with one small step. The second step becomes easier as does the third and fourth. The important part is that you keep stepping. The most important thing we can do for our health is keep our emotional state clean and healthy. The time is now to jump into the process and integrate new habits that will create the new you.

Case Study:

When I returned to my practice I was determined to utilize all I had learned to heal my patients emotionally as well as physically. One of my first patients had been referred to me by a friend who was a massage therapist. The patient was completely disabled, her spinal pain so intense that she could only stand for 30 minutes and sit for only 5 to 10 minutes before she had to lie down. I utilized muscle testing to determine the epicenter or origin of her pain as well as to find the emotional dynamic that encapsulated the issue that was causing her the disabling pain. There were three interconnected issues, abandonment, the fear of being alone, and a sense of impending doom. I asked her when she might have felt these issues most recently. She immediately told me how she had lost her husband, a policeman who was shot and killed in the line of duty. Her lower back pain developed shortly after his death. The pain continued at that level even when her son, who had also become a policeman, had sustained a non-life-threatening shot to his body. Ironically, after her son had healed from that injury and returned back to work, her pain elevated dramatically. In both of these instances she was informed that her husband and son had been shot via a phone call.

It was then that I needed to determine the initial sensitizing event which had triggered this emotional response. I asked if she had experienced a similar event earlier in her life and she began to cry. She explained that her father, a police officer, was also killed in the line of duty. She remembered her father leaving to go to work and then later her receiving a phone call. Unfortunately, she was the one who picked up the phone and was told by the commanding officer of the tragic event. At age 6 she was unable to cope with this inconceivable loss. It shattered her sense of stability and the belief that good things in life do happen. Who would protect her, shelter her, and most importantly love her? She felt alone and abandoned. The reason her pain did not increase until after her son went back to work was that while he was at home she did not fear the impending doom of a phone call telling of another great loss in her life. There is little question in my mind that she chose to marry a police officer because the issues with her father's death had been unresolved, and she would be given the circumstances that would force her to deal with this triad of emotional issues.

When the session was over, I asked her if she realized that she had been sitting and talking for over two hours without pain. She was flabbergasted. I gave her exercises for becoming more aware of when her emotional dynamics were triggered, and how to evolve her actions by doing the opposite. I received a call a few days later telling me she was in pain. I asked, "What happened?" She told me that she had been gardening for two days and that she was extremely sore from using muscles she hadn't used for years. I had a great sigh of relief and we both laughed. She was the perfect client to always remind me how powerful emotional work can be. I had treated so many people with practical adjustments, muscle work and stretching; however, in this particular case I did none of those and she was pain free. I became so aware of how emotional worry and stress and the processing of those issues can create disabling pain as well as detrimental dysfunction in the cells, organs, and tissues of our bodies. Once again, the salient message is that we play the most important part in how we choose to create the experience of our life, the amount of stress we have, and our own health.

The Best Road For You:

Now as you are learning about this program you've had a multitude of events take place in your life which brought you to a crossroads. The question is what are your choices? What triggers stress in your life? How will you cope with life? What is the healthiest path? What path will bring you joy? What is it that you fear? What can you do to change my current path? Unfortunately we often just let life happen to us without taking control. This rarely leads to a harmonious path, because we continue to do the same thing we have always done, never growing or evolving. We are creatures of habit. The trick is to initiate a new change of actions and thoughts that will put you on a completely new path. It's really quite simple even though you may fear change, enlightened change is what will allow you to grow and maintain your health.

Let's acknowledge the pitfalls right now that are so easy to fall into. First, is **denial,** telling oneself that everything is okay and there is no need to change. This allows you to continue on a path of solidifying actions that create your stress and disease. It is the first step in a downward spiral. The next is **self-medication** with drugs including coffee, alcohol, recreational marijuana, and other drugs and addictions that dull the senses. Self-medication can take many forms, but all have the common thread of distraction. Even using exercise to reduce tensions may be indicative of a disharmonious path. Although exercise is necessary to overall health, it cannot take the place of strengthening one's emotional core. You may fear change, but creating self-awareness through a harmonizing process will allow the growth necessary to lead to one's best health. The answer to how to derail this downward cycle is to admit and deeply investigate the emotional issues that cause stress. We must all recognize and face our fears and weaknesses, and admit that we have done something bad. This is the greatest fear of the ego.

Our Controlling Ego:

Our ego is often referred to as a person's sense of self-esteem or self-importance. It is the part of the mind that mediates between the conscious and the unconscious. Our ego is responsible for our sense of personal identity. We want to feel good about ourselves. This part of our conscious mind has both healthful and unhealthful traits. For most of us, it is the ego that gets us up in the morning and gets us off to work so that we can make money, and provide for ourselves and family. It thrives on the acquisition of material wealth and prestige; it pushes us to be active and drives us to compete in the world of work, sports, finance, and other aspects of society. It is the motivation that most people use to run their lives. The problem comes when the ego tries to remedy what it fears—failure. The ego will find a behavior that mitigates or rationalizes the feelings of fear or guilt which create stress for just one moment, then will carry on with that destructive behavior. This is the beginning of addictions to certain actions and potentially to obsessive-compulsive behavior. If a little bit is good, then a whole lot more is better.

Imagine for a moment a young girl whose parents only give her love and positive reinforcement when she keeps her room clean and does chores cleaning around the house. The probable outcome of this will be a woman who is a cleaning machine. She will spend every moment cleaning things around the house and might decide to become a professional housecleaner. She will constantly be seeking approval through the act of keeping clean and doing chores. If this issue goes unaddressed, it will stop being functional and become an obsession. This person will need to have everything perfect and clean and never allow children to play outside where they might bring in dirt. She will never have a fire in the fireplace. That would require carrying in wood and it could possibly smoke. It will become hard for that person to rest and just watch TV when there are things that could be cleaned. If anything in her home is not clean, she is stressed. Having a spotless home is how she feels self-worth and at peace. This is just one example of how an unaddressed issue can become a neurotic and obsessive behavior. This is a true case history.

The ego believes in survival of the fittest and will always put you first. Its greatest strategy is to try to lift you up while putting other people down. It never wants to put itself in a situation where it confronts its greatest fear—the feeling of not being good enough! An easy example of this is a bully who only picks on the weak. The more insidious and universal examples of this are in the comparison of power, looks, money, intellect, strength, and wealth. It is pride and the ego that are responsible for damaging gossip and contention even to the extent of war. Negatively comparing ourselves to others is the cause of our feelings of stress, anger, betrayal, insecurity, envy and other emotions. This is part of the human hard-drive, which is the core to our very existence.

Our Guiding Soul:

Lucky for us there is a stronger guide, perhaps a divine spark within us that patiently, calmly, and with great resolve helps us connect to our humanity. I see this as our soul. It is our innate, inherited instinct to know that when we treat others with kindness we feel good inside. It is this knowledge that has created the golden rule for every religion of the world: "Do unto others as you would have them do unto you." Perhaps what this is really saying is, "Do unto others as you are doing unto yourself." This knowledge that we are all interconnected and that our actions have implications to all that surrounds us, passionately motivates us to consider the needs and feelings of others. We know that in some way how we treat others will have a direct effect on ourselves. Remember the soul is a part of you that is always there. It is the little voice that always rings true. The more you learn to put your ego to the side, the louder the soul's voice will become. So let's talk about how we start our journey along that path.

The Steps of your Harmonious Evolution:

- **Awaken**: The first step in evolution is to **awaken** to the fact that there is an issue. That is to say that you are dealing with an emotional dynamic that brings you stress. The symptoms of this might be anger towards people, frustration with how the world is going, a general sense of negativity, high blood pressure or heart rate especially when you are in certain situations or around certain people.

- **Remembrance or self-examination**: The next step is **remembrance**. This is the stage when you connect with who you are, who you are meant to be, what life might be like without these issues, and perhaps access more of that wise internal voice. To be at the point of remembrance, you have to awaken to the reality that you have a problem and own it. There is no more denial, fantasy or diversion. Self-examination reminds you of who you are and who you can be.

- **Awareness:** Next is **awareness**. In this stage you will become fully aware of the emotional dynamic you're dealing with. You will begin to see how this issue shows up in so many of your actions. You will even begin to see how most of these dysfunctional actions are created to combat or avoid your fears. It is a good idea to carry a journal where you can write down every instance of when you confronted the emotional dynamic or issue. It is also important to write down answers to these questions: 1. Are you continuing to react the same way? 2. If you repeated your usual action, how will you do it differently the next time you are confronted with the same issue? 3. If you did it differently, what did you do and what were the results—positive or negative?

  In the beginning of this practice it may be difficult to see how invasive beliefs and their actions are in what you do day-after-day. Stay with it and continue to work with the motivations for your actions and over time you will find that the main emotional issues of your life affect nearly every decision you make. It is here that you will not only grow tired of seeing this issue over and over again, but it will begin to sicken you to see how much this issue controls your life. At this point, most of the work is done.

- **Transition:** This stage takes place when you make the simple choice to no longer have the same knee-jerk response or addiction to stress that you have had in the past. You listen to your conscience or soul, review how to transform moments when you have taken action that was unharmonious and ultimately did not serve you or those around you well. As you actively listen, you will become more and more aware of those things in your life which need to be worked on. The obvious signs of the issues needing attention will be feelings of stress, frustration, higher blood pressure, or frequently thinking about something you or someone else did at some point.

It is important to acknowledge your role in the action and talk to the people involved. First you need to tell them when the incident occurred and restate to them what it was that you said or did. Next explain to them your motivations and the fears they came from.

Then tell them what you wish you had said or done and would do today. Finally, you let them know that you are sorry.

For example: Communicate with that person no matter how long ago the occurrence was and tell them the following:

1. "There was a time when I said or did something that I am not proud of, (happy about, or regret.") Use whichever is most appropriate.
2. Explain the incident.
3. "I understand now that these were my motivations. . ." It is important that you expose the true roots of your fear in this step. You will of course expose more with those that you love and who love you. What you will see and feel after opening up is that you are the same person and that there is great strength in being able to be truthful. After the first time doing this it becomes easier and easier. It is in this action that most people hear you and their feelings about your past actions soften.

    The description of your motivations can be as simple as saying, "I have a fear of being controlled." You can also go a little deeper depending upon who you're talking to. This builds your strength and growth in dealing with these issues. This is very important because talking about these fears freely and openly, desensitizes them. You'll discover your inner strength as you can talk while not being fearful. Many times the people you have had unharmonious actions with will be angry and not wish to talk to you. This is sometimes the punishment that their ego wishes. If you are looking for a guideline of how many times you should try contacting them to get this information across, I believe the answer is three times. This is a good time to go even deeper and look for additional layers in each of the times you try to contact them to see if there is more to it than just the first thing you felt you needed to harmonize.

4. The next step is to tell them, "If I could do it again today, this is how I would do it differently."
5. Finally tell them, "I hope you will hear me," or whatever is most appropriate for the situation.

    Throughout these steps, it is imperative that you express your true feelings, but never enlist name-calling, blame or the word YOU. For example, instead of telling someone, "When you yell at me, I fear that you will hurt me," say "Whenever anyone starts yelling at me, I fear being hurt." This keeps the person you're talking to from becoming defensive and open to listening to you with more understanding. It is important to show up, tell the truth, do the best job you can, and be unattached to the outcome.

    Here is a typical scenario: A husband might say, "Four weeks ago I misled you when I said I had to work some overtime and that we couldn't go on that business trip with my company. The truth is I didn't want you to go because I have had a terrible year in sales, compared to last year when I won many sales awards. I also don't like how my coworkers look at you. My motivation was my fear of losing you. I work so hard to provide for you and give you the things that will make you want to stay with me. With my sales so low I was feeling insecure and then to put you around the guys who are making so much more money than I am now, brought that fear of abandonment out even more. I know now that I have always thought that material things are what kept you with me." In this stage, he may even become aware of the time when he took on the belief that he was only as good as his material acquisitions. He may even see that these issues came from his mother or father or society at large. As with most things our issues will boil down to the fear of not measuring up to another's expectations.

- **Transformation** is the next step. It is here after you have done so much deep work that you stop attracting the situations you need to confront to evolve. It is interesting to speculate how this works: either your soul works behind-the-scenes making sure that you continue to confront time and time again the situations that are needed for you to evolve or the laws of manifesting are always at work. The main premise of manifesting is that you attract your greatest thought form. Most of the time our greatest thought form is a fear deep in the subconscious mind—especially when you're on autopilot and lack introspection. The laws of manifesting will bring to you the very issues you need to work on and overcome. It's really a beautiful system when you're on this path. This stage propels the continuation of the harmonizing path. In this stage you are very aware of when those emotional issues which would've triggered you in the past no longer have control over you. This is the moment when you will smile as you see your growth and know that this path is self-perpetuating with great rewards.

These are the steps that you will take in the active meditation offered in this program. Now as you expand the actions of awareness and transformation, you will adapt these transformative actions in your daily life with all the people in your life. Once you have completed this process it is easier to do it again and again with each of the emotional issues that create stress in your life. The path usually brings you to the big ones at first and then it feeds you the next emotional issues that are easier to work with. It is here that your outlook on life really changes.

The Rewards Are Perpetual:

I want to let you in on a little secret. This path is as old as humanity itself. There are many names for this path in many of the different religions, philosophies and psychological practices. I believe the most familiar name would be The Path to Enlightenment. The pillars of this path are that you are able to dig deep into the motivations for every one of your actions. Every movement in your life is motivated by an action that has rewarded you in your past. Many of your motivations and actions are positive and you will want to keep them, because they work well and have no negative consequences. The ones you need to allow yourself to recognize and address are the ones that create stress, disharmony, and disease in your life.

There are many more benefits to this path than you might imagine. You will give yourself the greatest probability of living a longer and healthier life. You will take charge of how you affect and co-create life rather than having life affect you. You may even realize how your thoughts and consciousness will wrap around all that surround you and begin to manifest life in a much more positive way. You will learn how to always create the best outcomes in your life by looking for the lessons you can learn and what you might gain from any circumstance that once would've seemed overwhelming. You will certainly have a greater connection to and awareness of the wise guiding little voice or divine spark within you. This will lead to fewer dead ends and bumps in your life. Perhaps the simplest and most enjoyable part of rewriting everything that once caused you stress is the absolute expansion of life. In this state you are much more capable of seeing the beauty in the world around you. The negativities that came from a stressful life, once reduced will allow you to see the world in a broader way. When you are not spending the majority of your time processing and holding onto all of your fears, worries and cyclic thinking, there will be moments of bliss when you will notice the scent of flowers, the gentle motion of a leaf being blown by the wind, the mindful taste of the food you eat, the joy in the sound of a child's laughter, or perhaps the warmth of your partner's caress. None of these things are ever to be taken for granted. All these things are to be enjoyed in moments of gratitude.

Understanding the Origins of Our Personality:

As intelligent humans we are not all the same. We have different learning styles, different reactions to stress, and different coping mechanisms. The vast majority of people were born with a primary personality, the equivalent of a software program to traverse life. It is a filtering system that predicts how you will view all of your life's experiences. You will see events in a predisposed fashion based on the belief systems of that personality. Everything you experience is processed through that personality's matrix of beliefs and emotional issues. This will set up what causes you stress and joy, and determine what you believe to be right and wrong.

In my years of practice, I have come to realize that there are four basic personality types. The different personality types uniquely prioritize certain parts of the brain to process all that goes on around them through the filter of their individual personality with its different beliefs and emotional issues. In the past we thought of people as either right brained or left brained, but it's not as simple as that. The brain utilizes both sides to process events, but it is true that each personality may have a more dominant side of the brain. This means that the vast majority of people who share one of the four personalities will have the same traits or issues they will need to transcend to find greater peace, happiness, and well-being in their lives.

Some people are born with both a primary personality and a secondary personality. In this situation your interpretations and decisions will be based on the interplay of both personalities with more coming from the dominant one. The situation can also dictate which personality will come forth based on the one that can best cope with the issues at hand as well as prior experience. The other way in which people have attained or recruited a secondary personality is usually through struggles and oppositions in life. It is common for another personality to be recruited to help the dominant one cope in such periods as work, the death or loss of someone close, feelings of insecurity about one's abilities when growing up, and countless other reasons.

Another way to absorb the traits of a personality, even though it is not the one you are wired with, comes directly from early childhood experiences including parental treatment. This allows certain emotional issues to be passed from generation to generation. A parent may utilize shame, blame, guilt, and judgment in trying to teach or discipline a child. This is one of the most damaging, however well intended, practices for a parent. When children receive this treatment from parents and others in authority, they adopt the belief that they are not good enough without question. Criticism, when used as a tool to control, will tear apart the self-esteem of the future adult. In addition to negative input from parents, children can develop a positive self-esteem when they experience positive reinforcement, gratitude, and unconditional love. There will always be a proportion of both positive and negative inputs from our parents. **Everyone will deal with issues of not feeling good enough on some level.** That is our target issue. It is important in this journey to be aware of this potential transference. Individuals who have not been torn down by parents, teachers, and/or society and have been given more unconditional love, and support as an interwoven presence in their lives as they were growing up will have an easier path, but not one free of issues that create stress. The recognition of the negative beliefs and emotional issues that you carry allows you to harmonize them and transform them into a new way of living. It can be very empowering to know that you have a choice.

I created the following personality test based on my research and clinical findings. The results will reveal how you perceive and process your environment, the personality's filter you utilize the most, and often the personality traits that you wish to integrate into your life. This information will give you great insights into your positive attributes and the issues you need to overcome to create less stress and disease in your life. Once you have discovered your dominant personality, you will be ready to begin the steps of your harmonious evolution.

How to Take the Personality Test:

The following personality test will help you pinpoint the generalized issues that pertain to each of the four personalities. It is important to take this test in a neutral mindset, like being on a vacation. A secondary personality might be triggered if you were to think of how you would react at work or in a stressful situation. There are 60 questions, but you will only answer 30 questions. The test has three sections, with directions that include an initial three or four sentences that will split you into either the first 10 questions or the second 10 questions in that category. You will do this three times. For each question you will circle the statement that best pertains to you in a neutral situation. If both statements seem to apply, choose the one that describes you the best. That may mean 51% of the time or the answer you thought first applied to you.

Later, you will go back and see the color that relates to that statement on the answer key. The answers will be denoted as R (Red), O (Orange), Y (Yellow), and G (Green). Tally up how many statements you circled for each of the different color personalities. This reveals your personality ratio. For example, you may have 17 G, (green) 9 O, (orange) 4 Y, (yellow). The combined total will always be 30. The meditation tapes that you will choose will be those of your primary personality. In this case it would be green. It is important to work with this personality first. If your secondary personality is close, roughly within five points, then you may also gain great benefit from the meditation session for your secondary personality. The secondary personality will come out usually in certain situations. It may be in times of tenderness or conversely when you are hurt or feel weak. It all depends on your life's choices and path. I hope you enjoy getting to know yourself.

E3 Personality Test

I apply logic to solve most problems.

I am very detailed oriented and enjoy knowing the inner mechanism of things.

I am good at confronting people when something needs to be said.

If the above statements characterize your personality, go to statements 1-10.

I apply understanding and consider all people's feelings to solve problems.

I am less detail oriented and prefer to work with things that are more artistic and creative than mechanical.

I prefer not to be confrontational. I am concerned with people's feelings.

I prefer to let things ride instead of a confrontation. Things usually work out fine.

If the above statements characterize your personality, go to statements 11-20.

FOR EACH PAIR, CIRCLE THE STATEMENT THAT BEST DESCRIBES YOU IN A NEUTRAL SETTING.

1   a.   I believe in traditional values and beliefs.

1   b.   I have my own unique values which often disagree with what others believe.

2   a.   I typically pride myself on looking for new and better ways to do things.

2   b.   I typically will stick with a proven way of doing something.

3   a.   I feel strength in working with a team of people and believe in the chain of command.

3   b.   I prefer working alone on projects without others around to complicate things.

4   a.   I prefer assigned work to be outlined in detail including expectations and goals.

4   b.   I prefer assigned work to be detail-free allowing me to expand the project as I see fit.

5   a.   I am theoretical.

5   b.   I am practical.

6   a.   A good answer is better than a good question.

6   b.   Pondering a good question is often better than a good answer.

7   a. My mind often thinks of alternative ways to reach the same goal.

7   b. I keep my attention on what needs to be done to complete a task.

8   a. In problem solving, I am excited by pondering possibilities leading to new answers.

8   b. In problem solving, it is easier to choose an accepted and proven method.

9   a. I consider myself and my thoughts to be mainstream.

9   b. I find myself and my thoughts to be different and more complex than most others.

10   a. I need to concentrate on one thing at a time when completing a task.

10   b. I can have several things happening at once when I am completing a task.

FOR EACH PAIR, CIRCLE THE STATEMENT THAT BEST DESCRIBES YOU IN A NEUTRAL SETTING.

11   a. I enjoy the present and spend little time thinking about the future.

11   b. I enjoy the present but find my thoughts drift to fun future plans and events.

12   a. I need to concentrate on one thing at a time when completing a task.

12   b. I can have several things happening at once when I am completing a task.

13   a. I can get lost in rituals and become disconnected from the deeper meaning of an event.

13   b. I feel ritual and ceremony connect me to the deeper meaning of an event.

14   a. I am theoretical.

14   b. I am practical.

15   a. I believe in traditional values and beliefs.

15   b. I have my own unique values which often disagree with what others believe.

16   a. In problem solving, it is easier to choose an accepted and proven method.

16   b. In problem solving, I am excited by pondering possibilities leading to new answers.

17   a. I dislike doing things that are repetitious.

17   b. I enjoy doing things that are repetitious.

18   a. I find myself and my thoughts to be different and more complex than most others.

18   b. I consider myself and my thoughts to be mainstream.

19   a. A good answer is better than a good question.

19   b. A good question is better than a good answer.

20   a. I take a conservative approach to most events.

20   b. I like taking risks and I enjoy doing things differently.

SECTION II

I would categorize myself as traditional, preferring accepted and proven ways of doing things.

Following rules is an important part of what makes the world function properly.

I am OK with doing repetitive jobs with predictable outcomes.

If the above statements characterize your personality, go to statements 21-30.

I would categorize myself as a freethinker or someone who thinks out-of-the-box.

I will follow rules that make sense to me, but the world is not black-and-white. Rules need to be constantly reevaluated and improved.

I prefer jobs involving new activities and constant challenges allowing me to problem solve.

If the above statements characterize your personality, go to statements 31-40.

FOR EACH PAIR, CIRCLE THE STATEMENT THAT BEST DESCRIBES YOU IN A NEUTRAL SETTING.

21   a.   I am willing to confront someone when the situation calls for it.

21   b.   I am less willing to confront someone. Things usually work themselves out.

22   a.   I find solutions based on everyone's feelings and input work the best.

22   b.   I typically find the best answers by using my own knowledge.

23   a.   I pride myself on being polite and kind.

23   b.   I pride myself on being respectful and honoring those that have earned it.

24   a.   I believe productivity and the ability to work hard are important qualities.

24   b.   I believe being sensitive and understanding are important qualities.

25   a.   I consider myself to be a logical person.

25   b.   I consider myself to be a feeling person.

26   a.   I typically give more to others than they give to me.

26   b.   I help people if they earn it or deserve it. I don't believe in handouts.

27   a.   I dislike conflict and look to resolve conflicts by finding common ground.

27   b.   I am OK with conflict and believe I can learn and grow stronger through conflicts.

28 a. I process feelings inside and do not like to expose my feelings.

28 b. I process feelings deeply over time and find great relief in sharing with close friends.

29 a. In relationships, I show commitment by providing and protecting.

29 b. In relationships, I show commitment by emotional support and comfort.

30 a. I would like to solve problems quickly but there are so many things to consider.

30 b. I am able to solve problems quickly through fast actions.

FOR EACH PAIR, CIRCLE THE STATEMENT THAT BEST DESCRIBES YOU IN A NEUTRAL SETTING

31 a. I enjoy brainstorming big ideas but prefer to give the mechanical parts to someone else.

31 b. I enjoy brainstorming big ideas as well as knowing the internal mechanisms at play.

32 a. I enjoy connecting to a lot of people and having a lot of friends.

32 b. I don't need to connect to a lot of people and can function without a lot of friends around.

33 a. I have no problem confronting people and telling it like it is.

33 b. I tend to avoid confrontation. It is hard to be negative.

34 a. I am more private than most people and work things out in my head.

34 b. I am outgoing and often use others as sounding boards for my thoughts.

35 a. I believe in morals but dislike them when they are righteous, rigid or used to control.

35 b. I define myself as having high morals and believe others should have them as well.

36 a. I see myself as an emotional being.

36 b. I am logical in nature and dislike emotions getting in the way.

37 a. It is the nature of relationships to come and go.

37 b. When I lose a friend, it affects me more deeply than most people.

38   a. It is not my problem when someone is depressed or in a mood. They will work it out.

38   b. I am compelled to help someone who is depressed.

39   a. I find it difficult to outwardly express caring and loving feelings.

39   b. I find it hard sometimes to contain feelings and compassion for my family and friends.

40   a. I believe being analytical and having skepticism is very important in life.

40   b. I feel good inside when I am connected and compassionate to others.

SECTION III

I am very passionate and active with groups and causes I believe in.

I tend to be outspoken and I enjoy meeting and interacting with new people.

I start projects quickly, believing that if problems arise, they can be worked out along the way. You won't get the job done if you spend too much time trying to figure things out ahead of time.

I rely on logic to solve problems

If the above statements characterize your personality, go to statements 41-50.

I have beliefs but I don't need to share them with a lot of people.

I tend to sit back, watch, and learn about people before I interact with them.

I like to take my time when making decisions or when I get ready for an event.

I try to solve most problems before I start a project.

I look to my feelings to help me with solving issues of life. I find it very difficult to work on projects when things are going wrong.

If the above statements characterize your personality, go to statements 51-60.

FOR EACH PAIR, CIRCLE THE STATEMENT THAT BEST DESCRIBES YOU IN A NEUTRAL SETTING.

41   a.   I see myself as logical and practical.

41   b.   I see myself as theoretical and experimental.

42   a.   I prefer work that involves brainstorming and expansion of ideas.

42   b.   I prefer work that highlights my productivity.

43   a.   I believe there is more *out there* than what we can see or touch.

43   b.   I believe in things you can see and touch. Things are either real or not real.

44   a.   Righteous moral standards cannot accommodate gray areas that exist in life.

44   b.   The world community lacks high moral standards.

45   a.   The health of the planet and all living things is one of our most important issues.

45   b.   Environmentalism must balance the needs of industry and the needs of wildlife.

46   a.   I see myself as a big thinker that loses interest in the details and mechanical issues.

46   b.   I pride myself on knowing the fine details and inner workings of a project.

47 a. I have my own unique values, despite what others think.

47 b. I believe in traditional values.

48 a. In problem solving, I am excited by pondering possibilities leading to new answers.

48 b. In problem solving, it is easier to choose an accepted and proven method.

49 a. A good question is better than a good answer.

49 b. A good answer is better than a good question.

50 a. I believe the world needs a chain of command and levels of power based on merit and hard work. This keep order in our world.

50 b. I believe in an egalitarian world where everyone is equal. Everyone has unique talents. The important part is recognizing and finding where our gifts work the best. If everyone were to do this, the world could reach its potential.

FOR EACH PAIR, CIRCLE THE STATEMENT THAT BEST DESCRIBES YOU IN A NEUTRAL SETTING.

51 a. In relationships, I show affection by giving emotional support and comfort.

51 b. In relationships, I show affection by providing, protecting and problem solving.

52 a. I am creative and often have a sense what people will like and won't like.

52 b. I am more logical in nature and I can figure out what people need or want.

53 a. I have my own unique values, despite what others think.

53 b. I believe in traditional values.

54 a. The best answers are logical and multiple input can unnecessarily slow decision making.

54 b. The best answer comes when you gather input from others beliefs and concerns.

55 a. I take a conservative approach to most events and use proven methods.

55 b. I like taking risks and I enjoy doing things differently if it pushes me to a higher level.

56 a. I push myself by "raising the bar" on my activities, appreciating efficiency and accuracy.

56 b. I enjoy creating with my hands. I don't have to push myself to enjoy what I am doing.

57 a. Usually, I can find all the information I need on my own, making fast logical decisions.

57 b. I enjoy input from others, and it can take a while to find a solution I know is a good one.

58 a. I am OK with change in regular small amounts, as big changes sometime backfire.

58 b. I am OK with big changes as it is exciting to see our ultimate potential.

59 a. I wish to be appreciated for my encouraging, nurturing skills.

59 b. I desire to be competent, efficient and accomplished.

60 a. I really enjoy multitasking, problem solving and pushing myself to see what I can do.

60 b. I enjoy doing one thing at a time and I cherish time when I am recharging.

E3 PERSONALITY TEST ANSWERS

1AR	11AO	21AR	31AG	41AR	51AO
1BY	11BG	21BO	31BY	41BG	51BY
2AY	12AO	22AO	32AG	42AG	52AO
2BR	12BG	22BR	32BY	42BR	52BY
3AR	13AG	23AO	33AY	43AG	53AY
3BY	13BO	23BR	33BG	43BR	53BO
4AR	14AG	24AR	34AY	44AG	54AY
4BY	14BO	24BO	34BG	44BR	54BO
5AY	15AO	25AR	35AG	45AG	55AO
5BR	15BG	25BO	35BY	45BR	55BY
6AR	16AO	26AO	36AG	46AG	56AY
6BY	16BG	26BR	36BY	46BR	56BO
7AY	17AG	27AO	37AY	47AG	57AY
7BR	17BO	27BR	37BG	47BR	57BO
8AY	18AG	28AR	38AY	48AG	58AO
8BR	18BO	28BO	38BG	48BR	58BY
9AR	19AO	29AR	39AY	49AG	59AO
9BY	19BG	29BO	39BG	49BR	59BY
10AR	20AO	30AO	40AY	5OAR	60AY
10BY	20BG	30BR	40BG	50BG	60BO

R = RED O = ORANGE Y = YELLOW G = GREEN

Dr. William Mehring

Work Space

Evaluating the Personality Test:

The personality test is intended to help you see your primary personality. It may also show you the personality you wish to move towards. The personalities apply to both men and women, however, they will have the additional influence of feminine energy. When looking at the personality traits it is important to add that component. The other variable is that all of us are in different places on the path of self-evolution. This means one person, often early in life, may not have had as challenging and difficult experiences as another. This man or woman may not have the intensity of the emotional issues characteristic of that personality.

There is not one personality that is better or worse. All personalities come with gifts and abilities that must be developed and issues that must be overcome. Harmonized people in each of the four colors (types) are some of the most amazing people you will meet, while those that have not done work on their issues may be much more difficult to be around. The intention of this program is to help you learn more about the positive attributes you can further develop and enhance and the negative attributes that may be causing stress in your life. It is important to remember that this is designed to create self-introspection and growth. In order for this to happen, you will have to be open to looking at the things that you do not wish to acknowledge, but may or may not have known to exist. This is your chance to create your new life and perspective.

In this next section you will choose the personality you scored the highest on, and then begin the Steps to a Harmonious Evolution by picking the group of issues that you feel would be the most valuable for you to work through. Once you have chosen one or more of the issues for the personality you scored the highest on, you can go to the second highest scoring personality and see which issues from that personality you feel need some work to harmonize. Since the intention of this program is to help you learn more about the positive attributes you can further develop and enhance and face the negative attributes that may be causing stress in your life, it is important to begin self-introspection. You must be willing to explore, discover and acknowledge personal attributes which are causing you stress and anxiety. This requires objectivity and a strong resolve to change.

Choose the program that correlates with your personality. The program will have a general group of transformative teachings, including audio files for downloading active meditation sessions that will help you discover and harmonize the issues of your personality. Although the responses and issues of each personality are generalized, your unique experiences and main issues in that personality will become clear. People with each personality type have their own issues and hurdles to overcome on their way to a healthier, happier and more peaceful life. These will show up the most in your relationships. You will be invited to awaken, become more aware, and begin the transformation and harmonizing process. There are, of course, many issues that are typical for each personality, so in the included audio program, work will be done on two of the major issues of each personality. You may choose to listen to both or choose the one that addresses your particular needs right now. This is how I have tailored the audio program to each individual.

Continued Transformation through Active Meditation Audio files:

One might ask why these audio files are so important to transformation. When one enters into an active meditation or hypnosis, the mind utilizes a different brainwave state that helps access and embed deep changes within your consciousness. In the hypnagogic state of active meditation you are achieving a brainwave state known as theta. In this state your thoughts are extremely focused and what your consciousness experiences as reality is weighted the same in the hypnagogic state as waking reality. This allows you to practice who you wish to be in this "energetic" reality before you bring it to physical reality. There is often very wise and profound input to the visions of active meditation from your subconscious mind as you are traversing these meditations. Do not be surprised with the information just allow it to help guide and transform you. The teachings and information that are being offered are best utilized on a regular basis especially when you are confronting the issues of your personality. There will be different layers of learning that come from the repeated use of these audio files from time to time. After you have learned more about your personality, one of the two audios offered for your personality may resonate with you more personally. It is best to start with that one first and then go to the second. Once you have experienced the audios for your primary personality then you can look at the sessions offered for your secondary personality. This will especially be true if the scoring difference between the primary and secondary personalities is minimal. The reason to look outside of your primary and secondary personality will be if you feel that you are working with some of the issues that may have been handed down from your parents in the early years of your development.

If you wish these additional audio files specific for each of the personalities and your transformation process they will be available to download at E3therapy.com.

The Red Personality: gifts, obstacles and transformation

These people are logic-based, responsible, traditional, structured, realistic, gregarious, pragmatic, and believe in authority with a chain of command. They are happy to work their way to the top—okay with a struggle. They enjoy competition, sports, overcoming obstacles, and even a good battle. Not afraid of confrontation, they say what their needs are and what they believe to be true. Their tendency is to be conservative and supportive of law and order. Their positive archetype is that of a warrior and a protector. They believe in hard work and receiving a good wage for their work. They are often the first to help others, especially friends and family. Seeing things relatively in black-and-white, "Reds" believe more in the literal translations of religion versus metaphoric. They believe in the value of a firm handshake. They succeed in leadership positions and are capable of managing people. They endeavor for strength and power in the material world. Although their careers are varied, they usually involve leadership, and power such as in professional sports, CEOs in business, coaching, farming, military service, contractors in the construction industry, medicine and the sale of pharmaceuticals. They are great at networking and the jobs associated with this ability. The red personality usually has little patience with excessive drama and excuses and feels that too many people are not hard workers and take advantage of social programs. Red personalities may find life more satisfying when they replace the need to win or be on top with appropriate empathy, or learn to compromise with the ups and downs of drama.

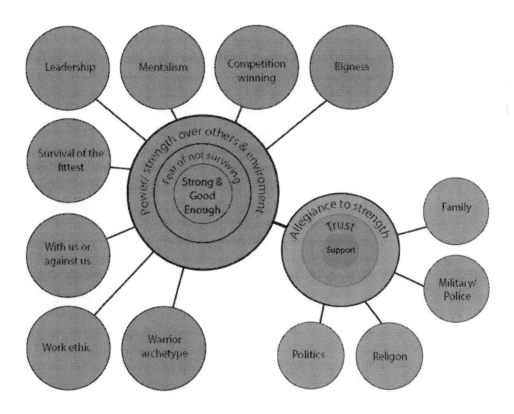

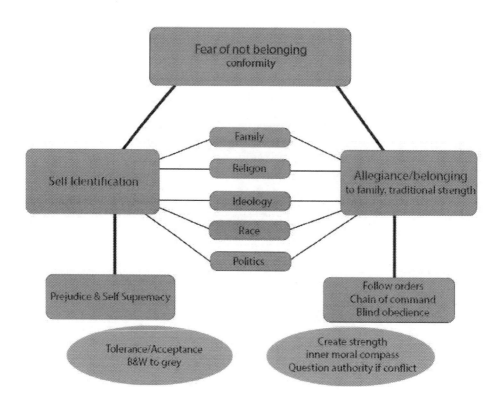

Dr. William Mehring

Red Balance Point

Minimal	Balanced	Excessive
No control of one's life	**Control & leadership** Not needing domination, control of other, work play, friends & family. Being okay with alternative opinions and actions	Control of other and enviroment Bullying, ruling with an iron fist, dictator, intolerant
Meek, pathless, non-motivated hides from conflict	**Conflict** Capable of confrontation & while being resolute & still finding compromise. Being able to listen & understand	Domination & submission
Over empathetic	**Empathy** Appropriate empathy	Non-empathetic
Anarchy & lawless	**Rules** Interpretations of law	Autocratic Literal, B&W interpretation of stringent law
Uncompetitive, unambitious	**Competition** Enjoys struggle, respectful & a good winner or loser	Competition Ultra-competitive, machiavellian, cheater, bad loser, hold revenge, requires domination
Poverty, reposession	**Materialism** Able to enjoy what one has Realistic acquisitions Purchases never to stabilize ones fears	Opulence, showy, heirarchy, hoarding
Laxity, permissiveness	**Acceptance vs. conformity** Tolerance & acceptance of others. In touch with ones humanity	Bigotry Feeling internal tension to differences: color, religion, sexual preference, & ideology (the new racism).
Non-religious	**Religion** Moderate- accepting of others religions & their path to god Religious text showing much about the truth of humanity Doing acts, works, service of religion Helping the down trodden Finding one's own path and connection to one's inner divine spark No hatred, enemies, vendettas Parables vs. absolute history	Fundamentalism Literal to self-serving interpretation of text Rigid, narrow veiw, isolating Resonates with intolerance, hatred & hypocracy

Red active meditation reprogramming (1)

This audio file will look at the fundamentals of survival and strength for the red personality. It will help the listener find balance with materialism, needs for power, concepts of winning and losing in competition as a metric for self-worth, balanced empathy, motivations for one's allegiances and how to stay on track with one's own self growth.

Red active meditation reprogramming (2)

This audio file will find balance in the needs to belong, be supported, releasing the need for conformity, duality and replacing it with acceptance of others and oneself. Additional work will be done with discerning the motivations for one's actions that come from fear.

Work Space

The Orange Personality: gifts, obstacles and transformation

Orange people are some of the nicest people you'll ever meet. They are very thoughtful and put others before themselves. They are comfortable with traditional values. They are very good at picking up verbal and nonverbal clues that allow them to read people. They are sensitive to stimulation from their surroundings and therefore have homes with soothing colors, music, artwork, and comfortable furniture. The guests of an Orange personality will be made to feel welcome and comfortable. They also enjoy having their own space where they can organize things in the way they wish to relax and recharge. Examples of these are shops, "man caves," craft rooms, and potting houses. It is a space where they enjoy creating and simply getting away from the needs of others. They tend to enjoy things that foster creativity and artistry. They are polite and will thank you for the things you do to help them. They are nurturing and great with kids.

Orange people commonly find their way into jobs that help others because their positive archetype is that of a caretaker. They make good social workers, accountants, nurses, psychologists, dental hygienists, musicians, artists, interior designers, graphic artists, law enforcement officers (especially when learning about their own strengths), woodcarvers, sculptors, finish carpenters, and animal or children care providers. They find satisfaction in working from home. The work they choose is commonly dependent on where they are in their own evolution. The less empowered the more they will look for jobs at home or that don't have a lot of responsibility. If they are pushing their evolution, they will be looking for a little more responsibility and oversight of more people. They are great at reading between the lines but sometimes read a little too much into what they think a person is trying to communicate. This is in response to one of their core issues—Worry!

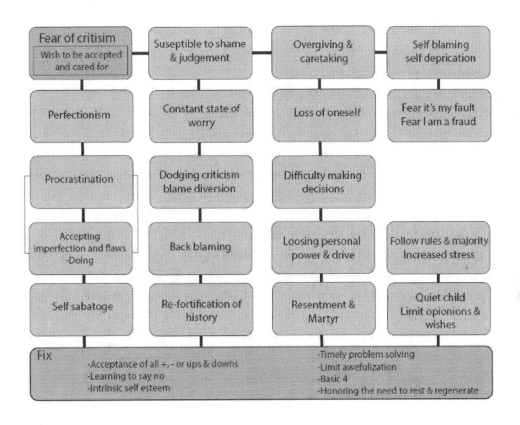

Orange Balance Point

Selfish	Balanced Giving	Overgiving
	Able to say no Able to ask for help Vocalize hidden contracts Reciprocal giving Being true & holding onto one's self	Put others needs first Shapeshift self for others Request others opinions on actions Difficulty asking for or accepting help Unbalanced giving = resentment Internalization = body pain

Excessive Self Worth	Balanced Self Worth	Low Self Worth
Narcissism	Healthy Identity Stands up for one's needs Saying how one feels Stating one's opinions Doing things your way with some input from others Self trust Intrinsic self esteem	How do others want me to act & be? What do you want me to beleive? What is my path? Developed facade to make others happy & accepting Endless need for others acknowledgment & appreciation Reflective self esteem
	The act of balancing to the above returns power, self esteem, decison making, eliminates takers, hoarders & the self aborbed. Finding soul print.	All of the above actions lead to loss of identity, personal power, the ability to make decisions, knowing ones purpose and passion.

Dr. William Mehring

Orange
Worry & Fear

Minimal	Balanced	Excessive
-Accident prone -Self & others -Doing without thinking & consequence	-Limits worry by awareness, acceptance, downgrading(talking one's self down), appropriate actions, timely -99% rule- same neurochemicals -Appropriate saftey & work ethic (basic 4) -No cyclic thinking	-Worries about every real & imagined potential -Never makes waves or goes against the majority -Strongly linked to fear of criticism or accepted ways. -Logarithmic "awefulization"

Orange active meditation reprogramming (1)

This audio file will help the listener find balance in over-giving, speaking one's truth, opinions, needs and not losing oneself to the needs of others. It will also give deep guidance to escape the fear of criticism, being singled out, not being accepted, the issues of shame, blame, judgment and perfectionism.

Orange active meditation reprogramming (2)

This audio file will help shatter the potentials for reoccurring worry and the awefulization process. It will give clarity to the roots of fear and self-sabotage. Additionally, work will be done on creating intrinsic self-esteem that is not reliant on the opinion of others.

<u>Work Space</u>

The Yellow Personality: gifts, obstacles and transformation

The yellow personality can utilize two different pathways in the brain. There are yellow personality people that are more traditional, conservative and black-and-white in their thinking. There can also be intuitive, spiritual and progressive thinking yellow personality people. This split in personality will come from whether their way of perceiving the world comes through the five senses and the physical reality of the left brain, or the more intuitive side of the right brain. Even with this duality in the personality, the behaviors and characteristics are still the same. People wired with the yellow personality are independent, self-initiating, self-motivating, self-respecting, as well as a strong sense of self-awareness. This diagnostic ability allows them to recognize their dysfunctional behaviors when they are on the path of growth. They are strong willed, efficient, ambitious, responsible, and logical. They enjoy finding multiple approaches to solving problems, and giving advice. Having a high moral belief system, they have no problem questioning authority. Yellows need to understand the internal workings of systems whether mechanical, political, social or economic. The yellow personality is wired to look for better ways of doing things. They enjoy proving their own abilities to the world and perhaps more importantly themselves. They have expansive thinking. They endeavor to be competent. They often examine all the potential outcomes of certain actions or situations around them and can see the most logical and efficient outcome.

The yellow personality that enjoys problem-solving is perfect for a multitude of jobs. This is the person who gravitates towards rebuilding companies that are failing as well as finding new inventions that go to the next level. This also includes creating political and social change. The change that yellow personalities make will be in alignment with how they're feeling about life, positive or negative, and how they feel they are being treated by the world around them. They are great engineers, physicists, mathematicians, lawyers, politicians, teachers, scientists, medical researchers and specialists, philosophers, revolutionaries, architects, and in the religious world monks, rabbis and priests. For the right brain yellow personality the religious world has much to offer, but they will not do it in a traditional way. The monastic life works well for their internal journey where they can search inside themselves for their truth and motivations of life. The rabbinic life has lots of brain candy because a rabbi has to search through the literature and look for the internal intent of the law and match it up with their moral compass of right and wrong. They are wonderful at being a judge and see this as a great opportunity. The priesthood can offer many of the same roles, but will commonly be involved in social change in the evolution of thinking. They are also good with animals. Animals don't have drama and they never let you down like people can. Drama also is too emotional, shows weakness, and can have manipulation embedded in it. They dislike seeing these behaviors in themselves and consequently in others. The yellow personality will just get on with life. Lastly, as artists and photographers that endeavor to be technically perfect.

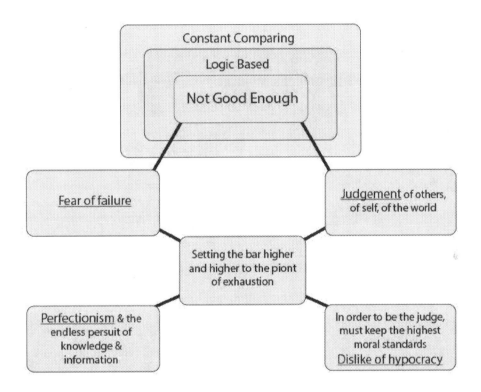

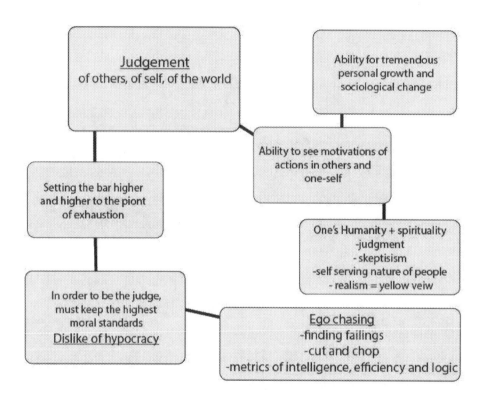

Dr. William Mehring

Fear of failure

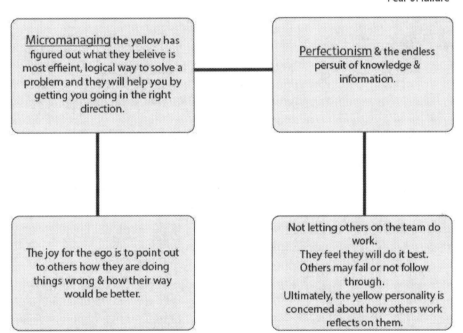

Micromanaging the yellow has figured out what they beleive is most effieint, logical way to solve a problem and they will help you by getting you going in the right direction.

Perfectionism & the endless persuit of knowledge & information.

The joy for the ego is to point out to others how they are doing things wrong & how their way would be better.

Not letting others on the team do work.
They feel they will do it best.
Others may fail or not follow through.
Ultimately, the yellow personality is concerned about how others work reflects on them.

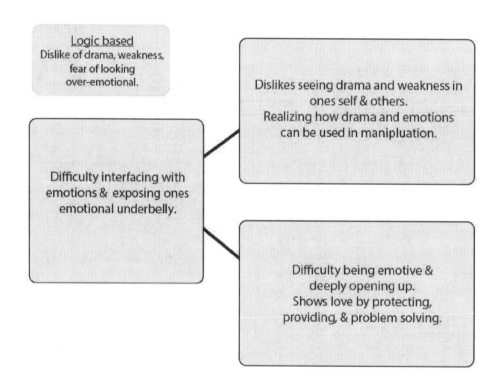

Logic based
Dislike of drama, weakness, fear of looking over-emotional.

Difficulty interfacing with emotions & exposing ones emotional underbelly.

Dislikes seeing drama and weakness in ones self & others.
Realizing how drama and emotions can be used in manipluation.

Difficulty being emotive & deeply opening up.
Shows love by protecting, providing, & problem solving.

Dr. William Mehring

Yellow Balance Point

Over Emotional & Sympathetic	Balanced Emotion & Empathy	Unemotional & Unsympathetic
-Overemotional -High drama -Mood swings -Volatility -Addiction to drama -Utilizing victim & martyr archtypes	-Ability to emote, express emotions of life (love). -Ability to feel, understand difficulties with balanced empathy. -Ability to support & confront. -Ability to let go of past & present angers without blame or accusations. -Learning how to process emotional pain.	-**Feeling safe** never exposing the soft emotional underbelly. -Having great difficulty working out emotional pain. -Always having the upper hand & control in relationships. -Talks without loving words or meaningful contact (hugs etc.) -Fear of judgment of improper behavior

Judgment vs. Acceptance

Over Accepting	Balanced	Judgmental
-Overaccepting -Enabler -Gullible -Fleecable -Unsuspecting	-Seeing indiviuals with unique gifts & struggles, appreciating everyone's journey towards growth. -Tolerance & acceptance of individuals & where they are in life. -No longer comparing themselves to others in the conscious or subconscious mind. -No grudges, enemies, profiling, grouping. -Everyone stands unique & unjudged. -No cut & chop.	-Hypersensative to differences, other's actions & uninformed changes. -All people must conform to the judges moral compass. -Isolates one's self with those they have issue with.

Yellow
Fear Of Failure

Not Successful	Success	Over Successful
-Inaction -Unmotivated -Minimalist -Lazy -Inefficient -Victim like' -Self disabling -Sloppy -Wishy washy -Compromising -Lets swing hard right	-Work hard, play hard, & rest well. -Okay with unforseen, or unavoidable additions to workload. -Goals only create direction. -Never compelled to start another job after finishing one (ego chasing). -Utilizing 4 steps. -Balance production with quality. -Okay with winning & losing. -Realization that life is not perfect or linear.	-Overmotivated. -Overachieving. -Perectionism. -Tireless reaching for success. -Always reaching higher. -Proving to oneself their abilites & not failing. -Never being satisfied with previous work. -Ever increasing efficency. -Acheive to exhaustion. -Overthinking projects. -Over organized.

Dr. William Mehring

Yellow active meditation reprogramming (1)

This audio file will help find balance between judgment and acceptance and the fears of failure. It will also delve into developing emotional fluidity, empathy, and finding balance in the needs for productivity, efficiency and self-worth.

Yellow active meditation reprogramming (2)

This audio file will work intensively on the concepts of acceptance versus judgment. It will also look at how to self-evolve through awareness and identifying each grasping action that is ego chasing.

Work Space

The Green Personality: gifts, obstacles and transformation

A person with the green personality has an intrinsic desire for connection. This is a fundamental gift and struggle. They tend to be gregarious, charismatic, relationship oriented, passionate, outspoken, and dreamers. They enjoy expansive thinking of the potentials of what could be and will always wish to be free in their thoughts and ways of living. This allows them to be a little more out-of-the-box and can be seen as disorganized in their thoughts as they jump from one idea to the next rapidly. Some may see them as having their heads in the clouds, but this is just an indication that they may be focused in the moment, or their thoughts are jumping from one idea to the next. They are creative, theoretical thinkers and enjoy brainstorming with others. They are energetic, exciting, and flexible. Most enjoy being the center of attention becoming performers, leaders and possibly the class clown. They are great peacekeepers and do not like anger, arguments or instability in their lives. The green personality can be very intuitive. They enjoy multitasking—initiating lots of projects around the same time—but are not good at completion. Boredom and loneliness are enemies. They have a hardwired need for relationships and are often very connected to nature. Exploring and expanding their experiences leads them to many different jobs, experiences, travels, relationships, and lifestyles. They do not see life in black and white and don't always see the rules as applying to them.

The green personality can fit in many places and careers. They will feel like their time is wasted unless their work impacts the world in a positive way. They wish to count for something bigger. Given their outgoing nature, they are also good at sales if they are driven by passion for a product. They make compelling teachers, coaches, trainers, leaders, CEOs, and animal-rights and environmental activists. With a passionate and egalitarian mind that strives for a better world, they typically find their way into changing the world person by person and as a human activist. Many people with Green personalities are hardwired to find their way into a healing profession. They will look for a practice that is unconstrained and has flexibility. Since they have great bedside manners, they choose a practice where there is more connection with the patients. They will be nurses, general practitioners, doctors of naturopathy, acupuncturists, chiropractors, massage therapists, yoga teachers, etc. Some Greens may become psychologists to help in a deep emotional way. The biggest difficulty is to have to sit and not move all day. Another place you will see a large group of Greens is in the world of performing arts. They are actors, poets, writers, dancers, singers, songwriters, filmmakers, directors, and did I mention actors and actresses.

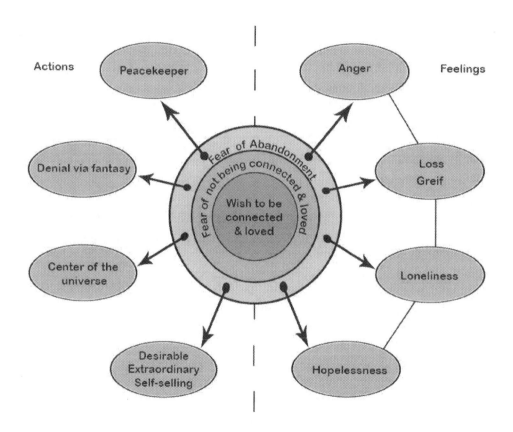

Dr. William Mehring

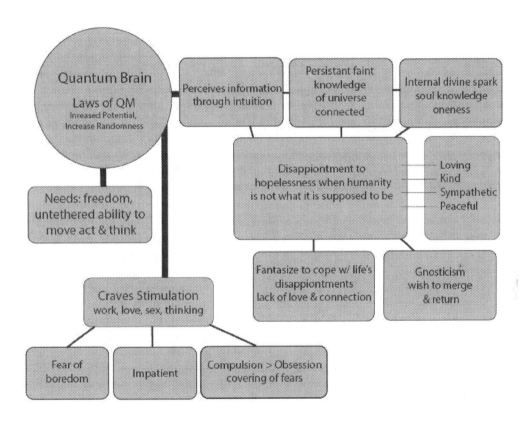

Green Balance Point

Minimal Connection	Appropriate Connection	Excessive Connection
Introvert Disassociative behavior Hermit Agoraphobia Distant Lacking passion/connection to self Despondent	Connecting to yourself, dreams, happiness. Embracing ones soul print & radically unique self. Never comprimising ones passion.	Losing ones soul print & lacking souls purpose. Accelerating degeneration & dis-ease.
	Okay with anger, chaos & superficial disconnection from others. Finding healthy 50/50 compromising relationships.	Being the peacekeeper. FOAb. Chaos ultimately disrupts connection.
	Harmonizing the need for connection creates balance in activies & relationships.	Enhancing experiences of connection & increased energy flow through extreme activites, drugs, sex, etc.

Dr. William Mehring

Green Balance Point		
Minimal Connection	Appropriate Connection	Excessive Connection
Introvert Disassociative behavior Hermit Agoraphobia Distant Lacking passion/connection to self Despondent	Okay with who you are never chasing extraor-dinary.	The tireless chasing of being extraordinary. Chasing aplifies the fear.
	Enjoying the ebbs and flows of new & old relationships. Enjoying the past without longing. Appropriate greiving.	Constant Fear of abandonment leading to feeling of loss, loneliness, hopelessness.
	Open to relationships with excitement but step by step.	Getting into relationships deeply & quickly (naming the children). Creating fantasy of relationships.
	Equal sharing of coversations & interactions.	Being the center of the universe. Needing all the attention to keep feeling of connection. Constant selling of one's self and over-talking.
	Being around others grounded in one's own gifts/abilities. Always staying true to who you are. Always being aware of actions motivated by FOAb.	Chameleon- morphing one's behavior, actions & beleifs into what friends and family want. Utilizing green flexibility.

Green active meditation reprogramming (1)

This audio file looks at the connection between the conscious mind, the subconscious mind and the connection to our soul. It helps to create the persistent universal connection that lacks fears of abandonment. It will help you connect to the little wise voice within, of intuition. It will help you reduce the loud voices of the ego that stand in your way of this deep connection.

Green active meditation reprogramming (2)

This audio file does additional works on the loud voices of one's ego. It will address the needs to be extraordinary, center of the universe, needing to be a peacekeeper, losing one's own identity in the need to maintain relationship/connection, seeing relationships realistically without fantasy, obsession and how to become okay with being "alone".

Dr. William Mehring

Work Space

I wish you the best in your transformations and that you find peace in what once caused you Stress and Chaos. To your health and happiness. Dr. William Mehring

Printed in the United States
By Bookmasters